CHILDREN LAW

Essential Legal Terms Explained You Need To Know About Law on Children!

DR. PETER JOHNSON

ISBN: 9781092437806

Table of Contents

Introduction

Thank you and congratulate you for downloading the book *"CHILDREN LAW: Essential Legal Terms Explained You Need To Know About Law on Children!"*

With a clear, concise, and engaging writing style, Dr. Peter Johnson will help you with a practical understanding of lawyer law topics about *children's rights, responsibilities for child protection, care and education, children's duties*; provide you a road map to navigating law on children rules and help you build a foundation for understanding the overall picture and **much much more**. This book delivers extensive coverage of every aspect of the law and details the duties a paralegal is expected to perform when working within law on children. High-level, comprehensive coverage is combined with cutting-edge developments and foundational concepts.

As the author of the book, I promise this book will be an invaluable source of legal reference for professionals, international lawyers, law students, business professionals and anyone else who want to improve their use of legal terminology, succinct clarification of legal terms and have a better understanding of law on lawyers. All legal terms and phrases are well written and explained clearly in plain English.

Thank you again for purchasing this book, and I hope you enjoy it.

Let's get started!

Children

Children prescribed in this Law are citizens aged under 16 years.

Interpretation of Terms

1. Disadvantaged children mean children with physically or mentally abnormal conditions, who are unable to exercise their fundamental rights and integrate with the family and community.

2. Street children mean children, who leave their families and earn a living by themselves with unfixed places of livelihood and residence; children wandering with their families.

3. Surrogate families mean the families or individuals that undertake to care for and bring up disadvantaged children.

4. Child-support establishments mean organizations set up to protect, care for and educate disadvantaged children.

Non-Discrimination Against Children

Children, whether female or male, in or out of wedlock, biological or adopted, born to one party or both parties to a marriage; irrespective of their nationality, belief, religion, social background and position as well as political opinions of their parents or guardians, are all protected, cared for and educated, and enjoy rights prescribed by law.

Responsibilities for Child Protection, Care and Education

1. The child protection, care and education rest with the families, schools, State, society and citizens. In all children-related activities of agencies, organizations, families or individuals, the interests of children must be of primary concern.

2. The State encourages and creates conditions for agencies, organizations, families and individuals at home and abroad to contribute to the cause of child protection, care and education.

Exercise of children's rights

1. Children's rights must be respected and exercised.

2. All acts of infringing upon children's rights, causing harms to the normal development of children shall be severely punished by law.

Prohibited Acts

The following acts are strictly prohibited:

1. Abandoning children by their parents or guardians;

2. Seducing, enticing children to live a street life; abusing street children to seek personal benefits;

3. Seducing, deceiving, forcing children to illegally buy, sell, transport, store and/or use drugs; enticing children to gamble; selling to children or letting them use liquors, beers, cigarettes or other stimulants harmful to their health;

4. Seducing, deceiving, leading, harboring or forcing children into prostitution; sexually abusing children;

5. Abusing, seducing or forcing children to buy, sell or use violence-provoking or depraved cultural products; making, duplicating, circulating, transporting or storing pornographic cultural products; producing, trading in toys or games harmful to the healthy development of children;

6. Torturing, maltreating, affronting, appropriating, kidnapping, trafficking in or fraudulently exchanging children; abusing children for personal benefits; inciting children to hate their parents or guardians or to infringe upon the life, body, dignity or honor of others;

7. Abusing child labor, employing children for heavy or dangerous jobs, jobs in exposure to noxious substances or other jobs in contravention with the provisions of the labor legislation;

8. Obstructing children's study;

9. Applying measures that offend or lower the honor or dignity of, or applying corporal punishments to, juvenile offenders;

10. Locating establishments for the production or storage of pesticides, toxic chemicals, inflammables and/or explosives near child-rearing establishments or educational, medical, cultural and recreation establishments for children.

Financial Sources for The Work of Child Protection, Care and Education

Financial sources for the work of child protection, care and education include the State budget, international aids, supports from domestic and foreign agencies, organizations and individuals, and other lawful sources.

International Cooperation On Child Protection, Care And Education

1. The State shall adopt policies to expand international cooperation on child protection, care and education with other countries and international organizations on the basis of equality, respect for national sovereignty and conformity with the laws of each country as well as international practices.

2. Contents of international cooperation include:

a/ Elaborating and implementing programs and projects, and conducting activities for child protection, care and education;

b/ Joining in international organizations; signing and acceding to international agreements in child protection, care and education;

c/ Researching into, applying sciences to, and transferring modern technologies in service of, the work of child protection, care and education;

d/ Training and fostering human resources; exchanging information and experiences on child protection, care and education.

Right To Have Birth Registered And Acquire Nationality

1. Children have the right to birth registration and to acquire a nationality.

2. Children whose parents are not yet identified, if having request, shall be assisted by the competent agencies to identify their parents according to law provisions.

Right To Be Cared For And Brought Up

Children have the right to be cared for and brought up to develop physically, intellectually, mentally and ethically.

Right To Live With Parents

Children have the right to live with their parents.

No one has the right to force children to separate from their parents, except cases for children's interests.

Right To Be Respected And Have Their Life, Body, Dignity And Honor Protected

Children have their life, body, dignity and honor protected by their respective families, the State and society.

Right To Health Care

1. Children have the right to health care and protection.

2. Children under 6 years old are entitled to primary health care and free medical examination and treatment at public medical establishments.

Right To Study

1. Children have the right to study.

2. Children studying at the primary education level in public education establishments don't have to pay school fees.

Right To Join In Recreational, Entertainment, Cultural, Art, Physical, Sport And Tourist Activities

Children have the right to join in healthy recreational, entertainment, cultural, art, physical, sport and tourist activities suitable to their age groups.

Right To Develop Aptitudes

Children have the right to develop their aptitudes. Any aptitude of children is encouraged and given favorable conditions for development.

Right To Have Assets

Children have the right to possess assets and to inheritance under law provisions.

Right To Access Information, Express Opinions And Participate In Social Activities

1. Children have the right to access information suitable to their development, express their opinions and aspirations on the matters of their concern.

2. Children may take part in social activities suitable to their demands and capabilities.

Children's Duties

Children have the following duties:

1. To love, respect and be dutiful to grandparents and parents; respect teachers; be polite to adults, love the minors and unite with their friends; help the elderly, the defective and disabled people and people with difficulties, according to their capabilities;

2. To study diligently, to keep hygiene, do physical exercises, observe public order and traffic safety, protect public properties, respect the properties of other people and protect the environment;

3. To love labor and help their families do jobs suitable to their health;

4. To be modest, honest and ethical; respect laws; observe the school's rules; live a civilized lifestyle and build cultured families; respect and preserve the national cultural identities;

5. To love their homeland, the country and fellow-countrymen; have sense of building and defending the Fatherland, and international solidarity.

Things Which Must Not Be Done By Children

Children must not do the following:

1. Dropping out of school or leaving their families to lead a wandering life at their own will;

2. Infringing upon the life, body, dignity, honor or assets of others; disturbing the public order;

3. Gambling, using alcohols, beers, cigarettes or other stimulants harmful to their health;

4. Exchanging, using violence-provoking or depraved cultural products; playing toys or games harmful to their healthy development.

Responsibility For Birth Registration

1. Parents or guardians have the responsibility to make timely birth registration for children.
2. Children of poor households are exempt from the birth registration fee.

Responsibility For Child Care And Nurture

1. Parents and guardians are the first persons responsible for the care and nurture of children, giving them the best conditions for development; when meeting with difficulties which cannot be overcome by themselves, they may ask for help from concerned agencies and/or organizations in order to fulfil their child-care and -nurture responsibility.

2. Parents, guardians and other adults in the families must set good examples for children in all aspects; have to build their respective families into wealthy, equal, progressive and happy ones, thus creating a healthy environment for comprehensive development of children.

3. Parents and guardians have the responsibility to care for a regime of nutrition suitable to children's physical and mental development according to their age groups.

4. In case of divorce or other cases, the fathers or mothers who do not directly bring up their minor children shall be obliged to contribute to the nurture of their children till they become mature, and have the responsibility to care for and educate their children according to law provisions.

Responsibility To Ensure That Children Live With Their Parents

Parents have the responsibility to ensure conditions for their children to live with them.

Responsibility To Protect Children's Life, Body, Dignity And Honor

1. The family, State and society have the responsibility to protect children's life, body, dignity and honor; and take measures to prevent accidents for children.

2. All acts of infringing upon children's life, body, dignity and honor shall be handled in time and strictly according to law provisions.

Responsibility To Protect Children's Health

1. Parents and guardians have the responsibility to implement the regulations on health check, vaccination, medical examination and treatment for children.

2. Public medical establishments have the responsibility to guide and organize the primary health care, disease prevention and treatment for children.

3. The State shall adopt policies to develop the health cause, diversify medical examination and treatment services; exempt or reduce medical examination and treatment as well as function rehabilitation charges for children; and assure medical examination and treatment funding for children under 6 years old.

4. The State encourages organizations and individuals involved in humanitarian and charity activities to contribute to medical treatment funding for children suffering serious diseases.

Responsibility To Ensure Children's Right To Study

1. The family and State have the responsibility to ensure that children can exercise their right to study and finish the universal education program; and create conditions for them to study at higher levels.

2. The school and other educational establishments have the responsibility to provide the all-sided moral, intellectual, aesthetic, physical and vocational education for children; and take initiative in closely coordinating with the family and society in child protection, care and education.

3. Preschool education establishments and general education establishments must meet the necessary conditions on the contingent of teachers, material foundations and teaching facilities in order to ensure the education quality.

Responsibility To Ensure Conditions For Children's Recreational, Entertainment, Cultural, Artistic, Physical Training, Sport And Tourist Activities

1. The family, school and society have the responsibility to create conditions for children to join in recreational, entertainment, cultural, artistic, physical training, sport and tourist activities suitable to their age groups.

2. The People's Committees at all levels have the responsibility to elaborate plannings for, and invest in the building of, recreational, entertainment, cultural, artistic, physical training, sport and tourist facilities for children in their respective localities.

The material foundations reserved for children's study, recreational and entertainment activities must not be used for other purposes affecting their interests.

3. The State shall adopt policies to encourage organizations and individuals to invest in, and build material foundations in service of children's recreational and entertainment activities.

4. Publications, toys, radio or television broadcasting programs, artistic or cinematographic programs, if having contents unsuitable to children, must bear warnings or indicate the age of children not allowed to use them.

Responsibility To Ensure The Right To Develop Aptitudes

1. The family, school and society have the responsibility to find out, encourage, nurture and develop children's aptitudes.

2. The State encourages organizations and individuals to nurture and develop children's aptitudes; create conditions for children's cultural houses, schools, organizations and individuals to nurture and develop children's aptitudes.

Responsibility To Ensure The Civil Rights

1. Parents and guardians have the responsibility to protect children's legitimate rights and interests; and represent children in civil transactions under law provisions.

2. Parents, guardians or concerned agencies and organizations must preserve and manage children's properties and hand them back to children according to law provisions.

3. In cases where a child causes damage to other person(s), his/her parents or guardian must pay compensation therefor according to law provisions.

Responsibility To Ensure The Right To Access Information, Express Opinions And Participate In Social Activities

The family, State and society have the responsibility to create conditions for, and help children to access appropriate information, develop their creative thinking and express their aspirations; and listen to and meet children's legitimate aspirations.

Responsibilities Of Agencies And Organizations In The Work Of Child Protection, Care And Education

Within the ambit of their tasks and powers, agencies and organizations have the responsibility to:

1. Propagate, mobilize for, and educate in, child protection, care and education;

2. Develop social welfare for children, create favorable conditions for children to exercise their rights, perform their duties and develop physically, intellectually, mentally and ethically;

3. Provide child-care and -support services.

Responsibilities of The Communications And Propaganda Agencies

1. To propagate and disseminate the Party's undertakings and policies, and the State's laws on child protection, care and education.

2. To introduce typical progressive models, good people and good deeds in the work of child protection, care and education; detect and criticize acts of infringing upon children's rights and prohibited acts committed by children.

Responsibilities Of The Law-Defending Bodies

1. To protect or coordinate with the concerned agencies and organizations in the protection of, children's legitimate rights and interests; to take initiative in preventing and promptly detecting, stopping and handling acts of violating the legislation on child protection, care and education.

2. To coordinate with the family, school and society in educating children who commit acts of law violation.

3. The handling of children committing acts of law violation is aimed mainly to educate and help those children to realize their wrong-doings, redress such wrong-doings and make progress.

Responsibilities Of The State

1. The State shall adopt policies to invest in, socialize and expand international cooperation for development of the cause of child protection, care and education.

2. The State shall adopt policies to create conditions for children of war invalids, martyrs and people with merits to the country, children of ethnic minorities and poor households, children residing in areas meeting with socio-economic difficulties or special socio-economic difficulties, to enjoy children's rights; and policies to render supports for families to perform child protection, care and education responsibilities.

3. The People's Committees at all levels have the responsibility to organize birth registration, study activities and health care for children of families without permanent residence registration, right at the places where their parents are working or living.

4. The People's Committees at all levels have the responsibility to develop networks of schools, medical establishments, cultural houses, sport establishments, recreational and entertainment spots for children; encourage organizations and individuals to set up establishments providing consultancy to children, parents, guardians and the population on child protection, care and education.

Supporting Activities For The Cause Of Child Protection, Care And Education

The State shall support scientific and technological works, literary and artistic works, all initiatives and jobs done for the benefit of the cause of child protection, care and education; encourage organizations of all economic sectors to set aside part of their welfare funds or profits for the work of child protection, care and education.

Child-Support Funds

1. Child-support funds are set up for the purpose of mobilizing voluntary contributions of domestic and foreign agencies, organizations and individuals, international aids and State budget supports for the cause of child protection, care and education.

2. Child-support funds must be mobilized, managed and used for the right purposes under the State's current financial regulations.

Disadvantaged Children

Disadvantaged children include orphans having no one to rely on, abandoned children; defective and disabled children; children being victims of toxic chemicals; children infected with HIV/AIDS; children doing hard or hazardous jobs or contacting noxious substances; children working far from their families; street children; sexually-abused children; children addicted to narcotics and juvenile offenders.

The Work Of Protection, Care And Education
Of Disadvantaged Children

1. In the work of child protection, care and education, importance must be attached to preventing and stopping children from falling into disadvantaged circumstances; promptly handling and alleviating children's disadvantaged circumstances; constantly supporting disadvantaged children in health and mental restoration and moral education; detecting, preventing and promptly handling acts of letting children fall into disadvantaged circumstances.

2. The care for and nurture of disadvantaged children shall be carried out mainly at their families or surrogate families. The care for and nurture of disadvantaged children in child-support establishments shall only apply to those children who are not cared for, or brought up in their families or surrogate families.

3. To create conditions for disadvantaged children to study at schools or special education establishments.

State's Policies Towards Disadvantaged Children

1. The State shall adopt policies to create conditions for disadvantaged children to enjoy children's rights; support individuals and families that undertake to care for and bring up children; encourage organizations and individuals to support children or set up child-support establishments in order to ensure that all disadvantaged children having no one to rely on be cared for and brought up.

2. The People's Committees at all levels have the responsibility to organize the care for, and nurture of, disadvantaged children at their families, surrogate families or public/non-public child-support establishments.

3. The concerned ministries and branches have the responsibility to provide professional guidance for child-support establishments in handling and alleviating children's disadvantaged circumstances, restoring their health or mental conditions and providing moral education to them.

Forms Of Support For Disadvantaged Children

Forms of support for disadvantaged children include:

1. Voluntary contributions in cash or kind;

2. Adopting, sponsoring or acting as surrogate families to take care of, and bring up, disadvantaged children;

3. Taking part in the care for, and nurture of, disadvantaged children;

4. Organizing activities to help children alleviate their disadvantaged circumstances, restore their health or mental conditions, and providing them moral education for them.

Conditions For Setting Up Child-Support Establishments

Agencies, organizations and individuals that wish to set up child-support establishments have to meet the following conditions:

1. Their material foundations and equipment are suitable to the contents of child support activities;

2. Their personnel have professional qualifications suitable to the contents of child-support activities;

3. Their financial sources are capable of covering expenses for child-support activities.

Operation Funding Of Establishments Supporting Disadvantaged Children

The operation funding of establishments supporting disadvantaged children includes:

1. The State budget allocations for public child-support establishments;

2. Self-procured sources of agencies, organizations or individuals setting up child-support establishments;

3. Supports from domestic and foreign agencies, organizations and individuals;

4. Contributions from families and relatives of disadvantaged children;

5. Other lawful revenue sources.

Service Activities Of Child-Support Establishments

1. Child-support establishments that provide on-demand services on function rehabilitation, drug detoxification, HIV/AIDS treatment or vocational training for juvenile offenders; upbringing of children addicted to narcotics or infected with HIV/AIDS, and other services on demand, may collect service charges according to regulations or contractual agreements reached with children's families or guardians.

2. Children of poor households that have a demand for the said services may be considered by the heads of child-support establishments for service charge exemption or reduction on a case-by-case basis.

The Government shall specify the service charge rates and subjects entitled to service charge exemption and reduction.

Orphans Having No One To Rely On And Abandoned Children

1. Orphans having no one to rely on and abandoned children shall be assisted by the local People's Committees to have surrogate families or organizations to care for and bring them up at public or non-public child-support establishments.

2. The State encourages families and individuals to adopt children; agencies, organizations and individuals to sponsor children or take charge of the care for and nurture of, orphans with no one to rely on or abandoned children.

3. The State shall adopt policies to support families, individuals or non-public child-support establishments that care for and bring up orphans with no one to rely on or abandoned children.

Defective Children, Disabled Children And Children Being Victims Of Toxic Chemicals

Defective children, disabled children and children being victims of toxic chemicals are supported and cared for by their families, the State and society; given conditions for early detection and treatment of their diseases, for function rehabilitation; admitted into integration classes or exclusive classes for defective and disabled children; and assisted in general education, vocational training, and participation in social activities.

Children Infected With HIV/AIDS

Children infected with HIV/AIDS are not discriminated against but given conditions to be treated medically and brought up at their families or child-support establishments.

Children Doing Heavy Or Dangerous Jobs Or Jobs In Exposure To Toxic Substances, Children Working Far From Their Families

1. The People's Committees at all levels have the responsibility to detect and settle in time the state of children doing heavy or dangerous jobs or jobs in exposure to toxic chemicals; create conditions for those children to learn or do jobs suitable to their health and age groups in their respective localities.

2. Parents and guardians have to maintain regular contact with children who have to work far from their families in order to help and educate them.

3. The commune-level People's Committees of the localities, where children work far from their families, have to create conditions for those children to live in a safe environment, be cared for and study, and temper themselves morally.

Sexually-Abused Children

1. Sexually-abused children are assisted by their families, the State and society through consultancy measures, physical and mental restoration, and given conditions to stabilize their life.

2. Agencies, organizations and individuals have the responsibility to undertake measures to educate, prevent, stop and denounce acts of sexually abusing children.

Children Addicted To Narcotics

1. Agencies and organizations involved in drug prevention and combat activities have to organize detoxification for addicted children at home or detoxification establishments exclusively for addicted children according to the provisions of the Law on Drug Prevention and Combat.

2. Detoxification establishments have the responsibility to create conditions for addicted children to take part in healthy and beneficial activities and make arrangement for them to stay in separate areas.

3. Addicted children being detoxified at compulsory detoxification establishments are not considered children subject to the handling of administrative violations.

Conclusion

Thank you again for downloading this book on *"CHILDREN LAW: Essential Legal Terms Explained You Need To Know About Law on Children!"* and reading all the way to the end. I'm extremely grateful.

If you know of anyone else who may benefit from the informative legal words presented in this book, please help me inform them of this book. I would greatly appreciate it.

Finally, if you enjoyed this book and feel that it has added value to your study or career in any way, please take a couple of minutes to share your thoughts and post a REVIEW on Amazon. Your feedback will help me to continue to write the kind of Kindle books that helps you get results. Furthermore, if you write a simple REVIEW with positive words for this book on Amazon, you can help hundreds or perhaps thousands of other readers who may want to enhance their legal vocabulary have a chance getting what they need. Like you, they worked hard for every penny they spend on books. With the information and recommendation you provide, they would be more likely to take action right away. We really look forward to reading your review.

Thanks again for your support and good luck!

If you enjoy my book, please write a POSITIVE REVIEW on amazon.

-- Dr. Peter Johnson --

Check Out Other Books

Go here to check out other related books that might interest you:

**Legal Terminology And Phrases: Essential Legal Terms Explained
You Need To Know About Crimes, Penalty And Criminal Procedure**

http://www.amazon.com/dp/B01L5EB54Y

LAW ON INTELLECTUAL PROPERTY: Essential Legal Terms Explained You Need To Know About Trademarks, Copyrights, Patents, and Trade Secrets!

https://www.amazon.com/dp/B07PFP3MDY

COMPANY LAW: Mastering Essential Legal Terms Explained About Limited Liability Companies, Joint-Stock Companies, Partnership, Private Enterprises, And Groups of Companies!

https://www.amazon.com/dp/B07P2PRVMJ

TAX LAW: Essential Legal Terms Explained You Need To Know About Types of Tax Law!

https://www.amazon.com/dp/B07PH1L3RS

INVESTMENT LAW: Essential Legal Terms Explained You Need To Know About Law On Investment!

https://www.amazon.com/dp/B07P79D925

**LABOR LAW: Essential Legal Terms Explained You Need To Know
About Law On Labor!**

https://www.amazon.com/dp/B07PFD2CML

CIVIL LAW: Mastering Essential Legal Terms Explained About
Civil Rights, Guardianship, Civil Transactions, Civil Obligations,
Civil Liability, Civil Contracts And Civil Procedure!

https://www.amazon.com/dp/B07P5GS8LD

LAW ON LAWYERS : Essential Legal Terms Explained You Need To Know About Law on Lawyers!

https://www.amazon.com/dp/B07PH9SCBN

Legal Vocabulary In Use: Master 600+ Essential Legal Terms And
Phrases Explained In 10 Minutes A Day

Civil Law Vocabulary In Use: Master 350+ Essential Civil Law Terms And Phrases Explained With Examples In 10 Minutes A Day.

https://www.amazon.com/dp/B0781TQWGV

Criminal Law Vocabulary In Use: Master 400+ Essential Criminal Law Terms And Phrases Explained With Examples In 10 Minutes A Day.

Administrative And Tax Law In Use : Master 300+ Administrative And Tax Law Terms And Phrases Explained With Examples In 10 Minutes A Day.

https://www.amazon.com/dp/B07JMD546J

Productivity Secrets For Students: The Ultimate Guide To Improve Your Mental Concentration, Kill Procrastination, Boost Memory And Maximize Productivity In Study

http://www.amazon.com/dp/B01JS52UT6

Shortcut To Ielts Writing: The Ultimate Guide To Immediately Increase Your Ielts Writing Scores

http://www.amazon.com/dp/B01JV7EQGG

www.ingramcontent.com/pod-product-compliance
Lightning Source LLC
Chambersburg PA
CBHW030729180526
45157CB00008BA/3104